Stories of Faith

By Brendan Murphy

Copyright Notice

More Information

Website: www.christian-ramblings.net

Email: comments@christian-ramblings.net

Preface

This book explores the existence of God through the miraculous works He performs. This writing is a collection of true stories from family, friends and my own testimony. God answers prayer to show us He is there and hearing how God works in the lives of real everyday people will be a source of inspiration and encouragement. If you have never seen God answer prayer, you will be amazed at what what you are about to read. These stories are a small slice of the countless miracles that God has done throughout the centuries. The apostle John wrote, "And there are also many other things which Jesus did, which if they were written in detail, I suppose that even the world itself would not contain the books that would be written." (John 21:25) Let these stories grow your faith that God is there and He loves you.

The works of God never come to an end, so another booklet has been added to this book called, "A Tribute to Our Father" written by my brother Shane. This is a tribute to my families' earthly father, but is also a tribute to our heavenly Father who transformed a sad time in our lives into a very beautiful tapestry. This booklet is a compilation of the experience of my family leading up to, and during, our father's final days before he went home to be with the Lord.

Contents

Stories of Faith

A Tribute to Our Father

Testimonies

In this world, there are many voices claiming to be the truth, but many of these voices conflict. So how does one know who speaks the truth? There is an inherent exclusivity built into the logic of truth in that truth can't be two opposite things at the same time. For example, you can't claim there is no God and there is a God at the same time because these assertions are mutually exclusive. This implies that there is no such thing as relative truth where one would say you have your truth, and I have my truth. It is like saying gravity is different depending on the person. If one person claims gravity does not apply to them, then asking them to jump out of an airplane at 15,000 feet without a parachute will ultimately test their disbelief in gravity. Therefore, truth is the underlying current in our lives that cannot be manipulated by our own desires and we all wrestle with what is the truth. So our real problem lies in recognizing the truth.

So how do we determine the truth? There are many ways to approach this question, but they all come down to determining the facts based on evidence. Without evidence, all claims to be the truth are like rudderless ships in the night. When it comes to the evidence of God's existence, one has to look where God does His work and these works point to the truth. The place where God does His primary work is in the hearts and minds of people. To open the door to our minds, God will perform miracles to demonstrate His existence and that He is trustworthy and true. These miracles are just the start of God's work for He completes it with salvation as He moves His hand to give the hardened heart a chance to listen and hear His words and believe them.

This book explores the existence of God through the miraculous works He performs. This writing is a collection of true stories from family, friends and my own testimony. God answers prayer to show us He is there and hearing how God works in the lives of real everyday people will be a source of inspiration and encouragement. If you have never seen God answer prayer, you will be amazed at what you are about to read. These stories are a small slice of the countless miracles that God has done throughout the centuries. The apostle John wrote, "And there are also many other things which Jesus did, which if they were written in detail, I suppose that even the world itself would not contain the books that would be written." (John 21:25) Let these stories grow your faith that God is there and He loves you.

Jesus on the Cross

Brendan Murphy

When I was a new Christian, I had a dramatic encounter with God one night. That night as I lay on my bed I could hear a drip, drip, drip, drip. I also kept seeing a post stuck into the ground when I looked at the floor. This was no figment of my imagination, for it happened several times and this puzzled me. The third time it happened I said to myself, "I'm going to look up the next time and find out where the dripping is coming from."

When the dripping occurred the fourth time I looked up. Suddenly, I could not see my room anymore. It was blacker than night all around me, and I was dressed in brown robes and I was in a prostrate position on my knees. What I saw when I looked up was the Lord Jesus and He had His arms stretched out on the cross. His upper body had great muscular definition which tapered down to His hips. His hair was medium length and had a slight curl. I was witnessing the final moments of His crucifixion.

The dripping I heard was His blood falling to the ground, and the post I saw was the cross He was hanging on and I could see the nails in His hands and feet. The only light I saw was behind the cross and as soon as I saw that light I said, "That's God!" The light was pure, soft, and white, and I could feel the living presence of God as I looked into the light and I felt His comfort.

I knew Jesus was watching me. He didn't verbally say anything to me, but I could hear what He was thinking. And as I heard His words, flashes of light would emanate from his head. The light was the same as the light behind the cross. And this is what He said to me, "I love you, you are my beloved son." He then bowed his head, and I saw His spirit leave His body.

It is one thing to intellectually know Jesus paid for our sins, but it is another thing to actually see Him pay for them in front of my very eyes. This experience changed me forever. It is hard to convey in words the depth of this encounter and how it became an anchor through the rough storms of life. When everything around me is screaming that there is no God or God has forsaken me I remember His words, "I love you, you are my beloved son." I take comfort knowing that what the Bible says is really real, and there is a God in heaven who cares for us. Through this experience God showed me that Jesus is His son and He died for me.

The First Time God Revealed Himself to Me

Bette Murphy

I was 21 years old when I had my first real encounter with the Lord. I did not grow up in a home where going to church was a normal Sunday event, but even so, I had a tremendous faith. I always knew that Jesus was Lord; but that was all I knew. I bought the "Living Bible," as it was easier to understand, and I was just barely beginning a walk with the Lord. I started reading and identifying with scripture and yearning for more, and yet my life was still made up of "the next party" and well meaning friends.

I was filled with discontent with the path I was going. One afternoon I was in my apartment alone going over all the latest events and I began to cry; my parents had just divorced after some 30+ years of marriage and my mom had just moved to California never to be married to my dad again, I was lost. I started to cry even harder; soon I was crying so hard I started to hyperventilate; the more I tried to breathe the worse it got. I fell on the floor trying to get air, not knowing what to do or where to turn. I couldn't call on the phone as I couldn't talk. I happened to see the $5.95 Living Bible on the shelf and I threw it open to the passage below:

> As evening fell, Jesus said to his disciples, "Let's cross to the other side of the lake." So they took him just as he was and started out, leaving the crowds behind (though other boats followed). But soon a terrible storm arose. High waves began to break into the boat until it was nearly full of water and about to sink. Jesus was asleep at the back of the boat with his head on a cushion. Frantically they wakened him, shouting, "Teacher, don't you even care that we are all about to drown?" Then he rebuked the wind and said to the sea, "Quiet down!" And the wind fell, and there was a great calm! And he asked them, "Why were you so fearful? Don't you even yet have confidence in me?" And they were filled with awe and said among themselves, "Who is this man, that even the winds and seas obey him?" (Mark 4:35)

At that very moment I went from flailing, gasping for air, to a deep sleep. I woke up three hours later and it was completely dark and I was afraid. I knew what had happened and I knew Jesus had been there with me. I looked in every room, and in every corner, as I was looking for Him who had helped me "quiet down." I never found Him physically but I knew He had been there just as He had been there in the boat.

God's Christmas Cookie

Shane Murphy

One mid-December evening in 1985, I felt that I should pray for healing for my girlfriend Mary, who later became my wife. I spoke with her and she agreed. She was afflicted with Hypoglycemia since the seventh grade and she was now nineteen years old. This disease prohibited her from eating sugar, which gave her headaches, dizziness, and made it hard for her to think straight. From the onset, it took three years before Mary was taken to the doctor to find the root cause of her headaches, lack of focus and fatigue. Wikipedia provides an excellent description of Hypoglycemia:

> *Hypoglycemia can produce a variety of symptoms and effects but the principal problems arise from an inadequate supply of glucose as fuel to the brain, resulting in impairment of function (neuroglycopenia). Derangements of function can range from vaguely "feeling bad" to coma, seizures, and (rarely) permanent brain damage or death. Hypoglycemia can arise from many causes and can occur at any age. It also sometimes occurs at random.*

Mary was very careful to make sure she did not eat processed sugar, which would drive down her blood sugar level creating headaches and the other symptoms. Her doctor warned her that sugar in large enough quantities could put her in a coma. Mary had some close calls in high school getting very sick after going too long without eating. The disease was an ever-present figure in Mary's life, a source of fear and nagging stress.

A month before we sat down to pray, Mary and I had received the baptism of the Holy Spirit (Matthew 3:11). It was a foreign concept to us since we found the salvation of Jesus while attending an Evangelical Free Church. Our church did not believe in such a baptism that was beyond being sealed by the Spirit of God at salvation (Ephesians 1:13). With the baptism, we began to learn of the gifts of the Spirit described in Corinthians chapters 12-14, including speaking in tongues, prophecy, words of wisdom and others. Healing no longer seemed to be such a myth of religion, because healing was like the gift of tongues, which we had already experienced, freely given by God. It brought a new excitement of faith to us. The Lord did not say to me "go pray for Mary," but it seemed right that we should go to the Lord with our request.

We went into my room to get situated to pray. She earnestly desired to be rid of the burden of fear that came along with this disease, especially as she would be heading to France for a semester of college in the spring. She sat on my bed with her legs folded under her and I sat the same way facing her holding her hands. It was a bit awkward. How do you do this? How do you begin? For a lack of a better idea, I began by using the gift of tongues and simply spoke in tongues softly for a few phrases. Then, I said out loud something to the effect "Lord, I ask that Mary may receive your mercy and that You heal the hypoglycemia in Jesus' name." Mary felt an intense heat in her belly and she began to slump forward. In my mind's eye, I perceived a darkness rapidly leave her body and exiting right out a window to the side of us. It gave me chills. It all happened in moments. I recall just repeating "Thank you Lord." Mary sat up from her slumped position, then leaped off the bed and ran into the bathroom. I wondered "what is going on?" She sat hugging the toilet ready to throw up. She prayed, "Lord, I hate throwing up. If its possible for this to pass without my having to throw up, please let that happen, but if its not possible, then that's OK too." The nausea quietly dissipated. She felt the peace of the Lord and she returned to my room.

Was she healed? We thought so, but needed to prove it to ourselves. So, we went upstairs looking for some food or candy to determine if Mary was healed. She would know quickly after eating sugar if our prayers were not answered. But, when we got to the kitchen we saw another miracle as strange to us as being healed; my dad was decorating Christmas cookies! I had never seen my Dad decorate cookies before, but not only that but he decorated a Christmas cookie by writing Mary's name on it! Dad knew of Mary's condition, and knew that such a cookie would be a cruel joke for someone with hypoglycemia. But this was no joke; there were no ill intentions, just the joy of the Christmas season. It became obvious to us; the cookie was a blessing from God, an immediate confirmation. Mary ate the cookie with no ill effects. She was indeed healed.

I would like to say that everyone rejoiced and praised God. But this was not the case. Some rejoiced, some were indifferent or suspicious, and others in denial.

We choose not to tell my parents. They were not especially keen about the whole "born again Christianity thing." My commitment to follow Jesus six years earlier at the age of sixteen pulled me into an evangelical church leaving my Catholic upbringing behind. Years later we told my parents as a testimony of God's grace and mercy. In the fullness of God's timing, this testimony was well received and led to a time of ministry.

As we told our closest friends at church, they were very excited and rejoiced with us. Oddly, some only reacted with "oh, that's nice." The church leadership was very reserved. Some people at church made us feel like we had done something wrong in receiving this baptism, but the evidence in our lives kept telling us that things were right. As a side note, our church later asked us to find a new place to worship with the understanding that "we agree to disagree" about the baptism of the Spirit.

After a month of very gradually adding sugar back into Mary's diet, we went to Mary's parents to tell them the news about the healing. Our news led to a tense conversation about how they did not know their daughter anymore because her Christianity had changed her. They opened the phone book and asked how many of churches listed in the yellow pages believed as we did, hoping for us to see we were lost in a fringe cult. Fortunately on the open page of the phone book there were a significant number of churches that believe in the baptism of the Holy Spirit. In the heat of the moment, they told us that if Mary did not turn from her religion that she could not live at home anymore. They asked us to leave and go think about everything we had discussed. Truly, there was no decision to be made. Thankfully, they never enforced this edict. Even many years later, I am not sure how my in-laws feel about the healing. The evidence is clear: Mary can eat normally, sugar and all. All the symptoms were gone. Every once in a while, they would ask Mary if she was still eating sugar. They were able to express amazement that I had no symptoms but could not acknowledge that she was healed.

My best friend in high school was very skeptical when we told him. I don't remember if he ever told us that he did not believe us, but he made it clear he did not believe it was the hand of God. He told us the mind is a powerful thing and that the body could have healed itself, or that Mary's condition was simply a product of her belief, suggesting the change was the self-filling prophecy of hope we created. My friend wrote a heartfelt letter to Mary urging her to go to the doctor to document the case, stating this would be best for all. Mary chose not go to the doctor to document the case. Why? It was clear to us by the wide extremes of reactions we received from those closest to us that it meant very little to them. Mary's healing gave her the freedom she longed for, and yet it had little impact for others. It was God's gift to her. Would my best friend believe if a doctor said it was unexplainable? Probably not, especially if the years of our friendship did not yield trust.

Is healing contagious? Several weeks after Mary's healing, I spoke with a good friend of mine who was also a Christian brother. He was an athlete and as part of his training he purposefully stopped eating sugar. During the off-season his plan was to eat sugar normally, but found it made him ill, like Mary's reaction to sugar prior to being healed. I asked him if he would like to come over and we would pray for him. He thought it was a good idea and he came over to my house that night. I had him sit on the bed, just like Mary did. Standing beside him I placed my hand on his shoulder, then I began to pray like I did for Mary. As I prayed, I thanked God for Mary's healing and I asked that He might do it again. At first nothing out of the ordinary happened. As the praying continued he began to slump a bit like Mary did. Then unexpectedly he violently inhaled and exhaled twice. It scared me, for he was a big man, but we continued to pray. Moments later he ran to the bathroom, like Mary did, probably as a precaution. When he returned he said he felt different. Time showed he was healed, and he introduced sugar back into his diet until he was back to normal.

What is the conclusion of these events? Mary and I developed a deeper appreciation for the personal touch of God, and his immense love for us. Mary was set free! God healed her, not to change the world around us, but to remove a burden from her. God, who loves the world, is fully able to love each of us as if we were His only love. This event in 1985 changed us forever, confirming our faith in Jesus is well founded.

Jesus on the Throne

Brendan Murphy

One day I was feeling down and slightly depressed, but a determination arose in me to not accept what the devil was laying on me. Every child of God experiences the oppression of the enemy, and sometimes you just get plain tired of the devil's constant poking. That day I finally got tired of it and I lay down on my bed.

I lifted my hands toward heaven and prayed. It began slow and soft; it was all in the gift of tongues. Gradually it grew more intense and fervent. I could tell the devil was trying too hinder me, but the more he tried the more fervent I became. This battle in the spirit went on for quite some time. I knew God was hearing me, and I was expecting an answer, but I didn't know how He would answer me.

The door was closed, the drapes were pulled, and the lights were off making the room dark. Looking in the direction of my feet, I suddenly noticed something coming towards me. It was moving very slowly, and I became terrified. Several times I said, "What is that!?" At first, it was like looking at car lights through a dense fog, but the closer it got the clearer it became. I was physically paralyzed with fear. I tried to move parts of my body but couldn't--not even a twitch! The fear was overwhelming.

Suddenly, I recognized who was coming towards me. It was Jesus and He was sitting on a white throne dressed in white robes draped from His shoulders to His feet. The right sleeve of his robe was pushed up on top of His shoulder making His right arm bare. His arm was strong and had great definition, and it was resting upon the armrest of His throne. There was a crown on His head, and He had an indignant look on His face. His eyes were aflame with fire, and I mean literal fire! The fire in His eyes is what terrified me the most. In that singular moment, I learned what it meant to fear the Lord.

There I was before the Lord, gripped with fear unable to move. I don't know whether He brought me into His throne room or if He brought His throne into my room or both, for I could see both simultaneously. As I was watching Him, I also saw demonic spirits out of the sides of my eyes. They were dull green and blue in color like sewage. I became acutely aware how they were hindering me as if they had grabbed my arms and were trying to pull me down.

His throne stopped a foot or two from the end of my bed, and He slowly raised His arm and pointed in my direction. He spoke a name which I could not comprehend and then said, "Release him." Instantly after He spoke those words, every demon spirit that was hindering me, with the speed of light, departed from me. My whole body physically shook and lifted straight up off the bed six inches into the air as they let go of me. An unusual feeling welled up within me as I was set free, It was like pulling up weeds next to a good plant, where suddenly the good plant has all the light in the garden to grow. My eyes grew wide as the Grand Canyon and Jesus then slowly lowered His arm and departed exactly the same way He came.

This encounter with Jesus on His throne is like what John saw in the book of Revelation.

> "And I turned to see the voice that was speaking with me. And having turned I saw seven golden lampstands; and in the middle of the lampstands one like a son of man, clothed in a robe reaching to the feet, and girded across His breast with a golden girdle. And His head and His hair were white like white wool, like snow; and His eyes were like a flame of fire; and His feet were like burnished bronze, when it has been caused to glow in a furnace, and His voice was like the

sound of many waters. And in His right hand He held seven stars; and out of His mouth came a sharp two-edged sword; and His face was like the sun shining in its strength.

And when I saw Him, I fell at His feet as a dead man. And He laid His right hand upon me, saying, "Do not be afraid; I am the first and the last, and the living One; and I was dead, and behold, I am alive forevermore, and I have the keys of death and of Hades." (Revelation 1:12–18)

Over the years, I have meditated on the times when Jesus has appeared to me on the cross and on His throne and why God chose to do this. One of the main things that was given to me is to communicate two different perspectives. The first perspective is Jesus as savior, and the second is Jesus as King and judge.

The first time He appeared to me He laid down His life to save me from certain destruction of eternal death. I felt great comfort on that day and He told me that I was his beloved son. The word beloved means "dearly loved" and since God doesn't play favorites that also applies to you!

When He had appeared to me on His throne, He gave me a taste of what it will be like for those who reject salvation and face judgement with their sins exposed before a Holy God. It is a terror with a depth that cannot be measured. What I experienced on that day was the most difficult thing I ever went through.

Think of my experience with Jesus on the throne like a baseball game where there is a pitcher, batter, catcher and umpire. In this analogy, Jesus would be the pitcher and the one who is to be judged without the blood of Jesus covering their sin is the batter. I was like the umpire who had an up close straight on view of what it will be like. I tasted a small portion then so that I could warn you today. You don't want to stand before God on the day of judgment without salvation through the blood of Jesus. Either you accept Jesus' sacrifice as payment for your sins, or you will pay for them yourself.

In our society, there is a reckless nonchalance that says the day of judgement is no big deal and we don't need to think about it. If you have been slack or putting off considering your eternal destiny, now is the time to consider the matter. Jesus suffered the wrath of God Almighty so you won't have to on the day of judgement, but you must ask for salvation. God has given you a freewill to choose your destiny. To say in your heart, that you will stay on the fence and choose to not choose is the equivalent of rejecting salvation. You don't know how many days you have left on this earth.

I know this can be a pretty fearful message to hear, but it can't be ignored that there are dire consequences for rejecting God's salvation. If you have been putting off asking God to save you, then do so right now!

When a House Becomes a Home

Bette Murphy

There are a lot of things that makes a family, but the most important of all is building your family/home on a solid foundation.

> "Therefore everyone who hears these words of mine and puts them into practice is like a wise man who built his house on the rock. The rain came down, the streams rose, and the winds blew and beat against that house; yet it did not fall, because it had its foundation on the rock." (Matthew 7:24-25)

I have lived on both foundations, and it is those lessons that have led me to where I am today.

During the most difficult time in my life I had one of the most incredible experiences.

One day while on my lunch hour, I was having a conversation with God, actually I was arguing with Him (in my mind, of course). I was walking out of the medical book store at the University of Minnesota, asking Him all kinds of questions: How was I going to make it financially, how was I going to handle being a single Mom with three kids, how was I going to just make it – one more day? The agony and pain I felt that day was immense. As I was arguing with Him, I all of a sudden heard a tremendous, "TRUST ME." It was the strongest, most resonant sound I have ever heard. What happened next was equally unbelievable; I looked ahead of me and there was no one, literally no one in front of me. There had just been dozens of people all around, I looked over my shoulder to see the very large open student lounge, but no one there either, I looked over my other shoulder and again, no one. My palms immediately became wet with sweat. A minute ago I was arguing with God, then He spoke to me, and then He cleared the entire area, so I would have no doubt it was Him. Whew!

Since that time I have built my house one board and one nail at a time on Christ's foundation. Sometimes I've fallen off, only to get back up and start in again, but oh how my house is beginning to take shape. The more I seek Him the better my house becomes. I hope the same for your house as well.

The Bible Study

Brendan Murphy

I was leading a Bible study of young adults of some who were going to a Bible college. Naturally, we would pray for each other and the Bible college students were well motivated to pray on their own.

Then one day, I was brought to heaven and I was standing in a field of rolling hills covered with what looked like golden wheat and I was looking at what appeared to be the sun sitting on the edge of the horizon. I moved my arms in front of my eyes to protect them, but I noticed it didn't hurt my eyes to look at it. At that moment a strange thing started to happen, what I thought was the sun started to move horizontally across the scene. At that moment I knew I was looking at the glory of the Lord! It was a pure, white, gentle light. The light streamed out like flames from a welder's torch in every direction. It was so pure and its fullness so great that I could not actually make out the Lord's form.

The next time the Bible study met I started to tell them what the Lord had done. They stopped me mid story and told me that they had prayed that the Lord would show me His glory.

There are times in life where we think the path before us is unending, or we have no idea where it is going. What this testimony demonstrates is that the end goal is God Himself. We are not here to please ourselves with momentary pleasures, but to put on the eternal perspective and live for God. The fact is that everyone who is saved will eventually see what I saw and more! In that day, your soul will be satisfied with the manifest love of God without measure.

Three Strikes and You're Out?

Shane Murphy

My second child, a son, was having a very bad night when he was only several months old. He was continually crying, like a classic case of colic. My wife was up with him trying to calm him down. She was rocking him in a chair in our room. I was trying to fall asleep but the crying kept me from doing so. After several minutes of crying induced insomnia the Lord spoke to me in my thoughts and said, "Go pray for your son." I was very resistant to the idea, and turned my head on my pillow hoping the repositioning would allow me to fall asleep.

The crying continued for several more minutes, and was becoming more intense. Nothing seemed to calm my son. I began to get frustrated thinking "will I ever be able to fall asleep." But, the Lord spoke to me a second time saying the same words again, in the same calm tone, "Go pray for your son." Again, very resistant to the idea I turned my head on the pillow and in vain tried harder to fall asleep. Yes, I know what you are thinking, "what a selfish man" and you are right.

The crying continued to intensify and changed into a pain cry. I buried my head in my pillow foolishly thinking it would muffle the crying so I could sleep. Several long minutes past, and the Lord spoke to me a third time using the same words, and the same calm tone as before, "Go pray for your son." This time I finally got the hint and obeyed. I got out of bed and asked my wife if I could hold him. She handed me my son and said, "I don't know what to do." I later learned she was minutes away from taking him to the emergency room at our local hospital.

I laid my son against my shoulder and rubbed his back trying to calm him. The crying continued with no reprieve. I could feel tension in my son's body. I quickly appreciated how hard this was for my wife. I prayed a very short prayer, something to the effect "Lord, heal whatever is afflicting my son. In Jesus' name." The crying continued with no change. Just a few weeks prior to this night I had read a book about Smith Wigglesworth, a Pentecostal evangelist with a healing ministry during the latter part of the nineteenth and early twentieth centuries. In the account of his ministry Smith Wigglesworth would chastise individuals if they would come through the prayer line a second time during revival meetings looking for healing for the same ailment. Mr. Wigglesworth made it clear that he would only pray once and then trusted God to do the rest, for he stood in faith that God heard his prayer. This example caused me to say to the Lord, "I have prayed for my son and now it is in Your hands to heal him, I can do nothing more." At the instant I completed my words chills ran through my body and in my mind's eye I could see a shaft of light come straight down from heaven encompassing my son and I; my son immediately stopped crying. With barely a moment passing I took my son off my shoulder and gently laid him in my wife's arms where he was peacefully fast asleep as if nothing had happened.

The lessons learned from that night was to obey the Lord, and trust Him even when you are immersed in your own selfishness.

In the name of Jesus

Brendan Murphy

In the early part of my walk with God, I was working at a place that makes awards. These awards come in several forms such as wooden plaques with laser engraved images on them. One such award model consisted of a four sided wooden base that had a see through solid plastic pyramid attached to the base with eighth-inch thick double stick tape. We would paint the bottom of the plastic pyramid black and then engrave an image with a laser to produce a raise image effect when you looked at it. After you attach the top to the base, it is possible to take them apart within a certain time period with some effort. After twenty-four hours, it becomes nearly impossible to separate them.

One night on the night shift I was working with a friend who was also a Christian, and we had to take apart one of these pyramids. It was well past the initial twenty-four-hour time period, and it was like the plastic pyramid was welded to the base. My friend tried with all of his strength to pull and pry this pyramid apart for several minutes. His face visibly contorted and his muscles exhibited tremors as he applied every last bit of his strength to pull it apart. As I stood there seeing he was getting nowhere, I asked him for the pyramid. He handed me the pyramid, and then I said to him, "Watch this." I held the wooden base in my left hand and the plastic portion in my right hand. As I was holding it, I could too tell it was firmly attached. I then started to say, "In the name of Jesus" as I started to pull the two pieces apart. I got halfway through what I was saying ("In the name...") and the two pieces separated with hardly no effort at all! I was standing there with the wooden base in the left hand and the plastic pyramid in the right hand as I finished my sentence ("...name of Jesus."). My friend's eyes lit up like a Christmas tree, and he started bouncing off the walls with excitement for what God had just done. I myself was standing there astonished at what had just happened and especially because of the fact that I only got halfway through the sentence before it came apart with no effort.

With God, all things are possible and sometimes we mistake adversity or difficulty as a sign that God does not see or hear us and we are left to our own devices to dig ourselves out of our hole. Walking with God is a symbiotic relationship. Like trying to separate the top from the base in our own strength we achieve very little. When we call on God, that which seems impossible suddenly becomes possible. In life we all face storms of impossibilities, but God is our ever present help and we need to call on Him.

The Resurrected Car

Brendan Murphy

I was attending a men's prayer meeting that met every Friday night. In this meeting the guys would share things and the rest would pray. One Friday, one of the guys brought up the troubles he was having with his Japanese car that appeared to be on its last leg. He took the car to a repair shop, and they gave him a laundry list estimate of $1500 to fix the car. The car was running really rough and was having severe problems even getting started. When we started to pray, I prayed, "God, I ask that you resurrect that car from the dead."

A couple of days later, one of the guys from the meeting went with the one who owned the car to start and drive it over to the dealership for repairs. They tried everything to get it started and finally after great consternation, they made it to the dealership. In Illinois, it was the law that dealerships couldn't be open on Sundays and the gate was closed at the dealership so he couldn't park the car in their lot. He had to park the car somewhere, so he pulled into the business next door to the dealership. He went into that business and asked whether he could park the car in their lot until the next day, and they were very gracious and told him it was OK to do so.

The next day when the dealership looked over the car, they found the source of the problem which was a small part and the repair was only going to cost about $70. After the car had been repaired, it ran as though it was brand-new and my friend was very excited about how God answered my prayer to resurrect his dead car. The real clincher that showed God answered my prayer to resurrect his car was the business where he parked the car at until the dealership opened and that business was a funeral home!

This is a funny story which demonstrates God does have a sense of humor and shows that He is approachable and full of kindness. He also demonstrates His wisdom in showing that even that which appears to be dead, can be made alive again. Do you have a dead relationship where you would like to see God breathe life into again? Perhaps you haven't been walking with God as you should have, and you feel the separation between you and God. You are just one prayer away from turning the situation around. In Jesus, there is hope!

Weather Stories

Brendan Murphy

The following stories relating to the weather are presented in the order that they occurred so that you may see the context in the last story.

Hurricanes just don't do that!

I went down to Denton Texas for college to become a professional trumpet player. During my first orientation trip, a hurricane was approaching the coast. I heard on the weather forecast that it was heading for the most populated area on that part of the coast. The friends I had just made had to return to help their families prepare for the hurricane. That night without thinking I closed my eyes and prayed, "Lord, I pray you turn that hurricane so that it hits the least most populated area on the coast." The next morning I walked down to the lobby of the dorm

I was staying at and saw a TV program discussing the storm. There were five weathermen lined up discussing the hurricane and what had happened during the night. I remember one of them saying and I quote, "Hurricanes just don't do this. It turned 90 degrees last night and hit the least most populated area on the coast."

Years later when the internet became a resource for the history of these events, I decided to look up what was written about the storm. Shown below are a couple of excerpts that talk about the events.

Source: Atlantic Oceanographic and Meteorological Laboratory

Hurricane Allen. August 9-10. 1980: When it was over the open waters of the Atlantic Ocean, Caribbean Sea, and Gulf of Mexico, Hurricane Allen was one of the most intense hurricanes ever. Allen reached Category 5 status three times. It obtained a 911 mb (26.89 inches) central pressure in the eastern Caribbean on August 5 while south of Puerto Rico. After weakening near Haiti and Jamaica,Allen again strengthened and a minimum pressure of 899 mb (26.55 inches) was recorded by a NOAA aircraft on the 7th when it was off the Yucatan Peninsula. Only Hurricane Gilbert with the all time low pressure reading of 888 mb in 1988, and the infamous Labor Day hurricane of 1935 with a central pressure of 892 mb were lower than Allen's 899 mb central pressure. Allen lost strength again near the Yucatan Peninsula but regained it over the open waters of the Gulf of Mexico with a central pressure of 909 mb (26.84 inches) on 9th.

The center of Allen did not cross any land until it moved inland north of Brownsville, TX on the 9th. Just off the Texas coast, **Allen hesitated long enough to weaken to 945 mb (27.91 inches), and then moved inland north of Brownsville bringing highest tides and winds over the least populated section of the Texas coast.**

Only two deaths were directly attributed to Allen. The strongest measured winds were gusts to 129 mph at Port Mansfield, TX. A storm surge up to 12 feet along Padre Island caused numerous barrier island cuts and washouts.

Source: Time Magazine

Title: A Monster from the Caribbean

One of the century's wildest hurricanes turns tame over Texas

Its itinerary sounded like something drawn up by a Caribbean cruise director: Barbados and St. Lucia, Haiti and Jamaica, Mexico's Yucatan Peninsula and the U.S. Gulf Coast. But the voyage left shattering death and destruction in its wake. Hurricane Allen brought savage 185 m.p.h. winds and 20-ft. waves. It wiped out most of the Caribbean banana crop, demolished thousands of homes and killed more than 100 people before its final landfall in Texas. Said Noel Risnychok, a meteorologist at Miami's National Hurricane Center, as the winds scythed through the normally placid Caribbean: "Allen has the potential to be the most devastating storm of the century."

...

Stalling off Brownsville for several hours on Saturday night, Allen lost much of its punch. Once the hurricane reached land and was no longer fueled by sea moisture, it rapidly subsided. Winds in Brownsville were less than 80 m.p.h. "Now it's just a ferocious little thunderstorm," said a National Weather Service spokesman.

...

"God was good to us," said Eddie Gonzales, a deputy sheriff in Brownsville, as the storm spent itself over sparsely populated range land. "It's as simple as that."

Green Grass

In the middle of one summer, a severe drought occurred and the consequence of this was that the grass in the yard was turning brown. If it completely goes brown, it will go dormant for the rest of the season. So knowing that God is a God who answers prayer, I asked God to cause it to rain in order to bring the grass back to a green and lush state. The very next day it started raining and it rained every day for two weeks straight and at the end of those two weeks, the grass was green and lush as I have ever seen it. Then the rain stopped, and the drought resumed as it was before. Through this incident God demonstrated that He listens and He has all power and authority and does as He pleases. This left quite an impression on me that continued to build my faith in God.

Split in Two

One summer an especially severe thunderstorm was approaching the house. As I was watching the reports on the local TV station and seeing the radar of the approaching storm from the west, I got up and went out into the driveway to see it. I could see the dark clouds approaching in the distance and without thinking I pointed at the storm and said, "I rebuke you in the name of Jesus." I then went back inside the house to watch the weather radar. Then something very unusual started to happen and the storm split into two parts right in front of the house at the point where the leading edge of the storm was when I rebuked the storm in the name of Jesus. It was like a perfect equilateral triangle wedge was placed at that point before the storm and the storm broke into two pieces and flowed to the north and south of the house. Again, God got my attention with this incident of how in control He is of all things. This reminds me of what Jesus did when He rebuked the storm.

> Now on one of those days Jesus and His disciples got into a boat, and He said to them, "Let us go over to the other side of the lake." So they launched out. But as they were sailing along He fell asleep; and a fierce gale of wind descended on the lake, and they began to be swamped and to be in danger. They came to Jesus and woke Him up, saying, "Master, Master, we are perishing!" And He got up and rebuked the

wind and the surging waves, and they stopped, and it became calm. And He said to them, "Where is your faith?" They were fearful and amazed, saying to one another, "Who then is this, that He commands even the winds and the water, and they obey Him?" (Luke 8:22-25)

And the Heavens Opened Up!

In the early 1990s I moved to Chicago and the upper midwest was experiencing a multi-year drought. For about four years it was pretty dry from 1988 to 1992. Early in 1993, I was up late one night at 11:30 sitting up in bed and without thinking I said out loud to God, "Why have you brought drought upon these people? I pray you open up the heavens." As soon as I had finished speaking, I fell into my pillow and immediately fell asleep. Falling into deep sleep like that was very unusual for me.

The next morning when I woke I remembered what I had prayed, so the first thing I did was to go over to the window and peek through the shades and I saw partly cloudy skies and little puddles of water scattered across the parking lot. At that moment, a sense of curiosity coupled with the fear of the Lord started to fill my mind and I started to ask myself what just happened. I knew what happened the night before was a supernatural act of God with the prayer because it was such an unusual thing to say to the Lord and how I fell asleep as soon as my head hit the pillow. With seeing the puddles I was starting to see something happen, but I didn't have all the pieces. After I finished looking out the window, I went to my stereo to turn it on as is my custom in the morning to the local Christian radio station. I hit the power button and a couple of seconds pass by as it powered up followed by the click of the stereo connecting to the speakers, and the first thing I hear is the morning announcer, with great joy in his voice, exclaiming the words, "And the heavens opened up!" To make it clear, this was the very first thing I heard when the stereo came on! I was a little taken back by these events, and I kept them to myself and I meditated on them. After I got the weather report, I learned it started raining a half hour after I fell asleep that night which is why I saw puddles in the morning.

Four or five days later I went to a Bible study. Between that initial storm and the Bible study, not a drop of rain fell. I knew God had answered my prayer, but I was walking in faith because I was being tested in those intervening days. At the Bible study I told the people there what had happened and then went my way. A couple of days later it started raining, and it didn't stop raining all summer and the drought was busted. In fact, it rained so much I got an unsolicited comment from a coworker saying, "It is raining to much." My pastor related to me that he found himself standing in six inches of water in a parking lot when he went to visit a friend at his place of work. He told me that because of what I said at the Bible study. 1993 was the was the year of the great floods that went down the Mississippi river. Another interesting fact I learned is the amount of rain that fell that year was equal to the normal rain fall for the four proceeding years of the drought combined when averaged out.

Warmest Winter Since 1895

In the fall of 1997 I was at a prayer meeting where one man shared that he was going to do surveying work during the winter. Money was tight for him, and he was concerned about the situation for his family. If it gets too cold, he won't be able to work and that had the consequence of meaning the difference between eating and not eating. This incident happened in the Chicago area and the winters can get very cold.

I told the other two men at the prayer meeting that God had given me an anointing over the weather (based on what God had done for me previously). After I had said that, both of them visibly scoffed at me. I prayed and asked God for a warm winter when we prayed together. I was put out on a limb and asking God for something in their eyes that was impossible, so after the prayer meeting when I was alone I asked God to answer the prayer for His name sake.

With this type of prayer, one can't tell whether the prayer is being answered until some time passes. In the beginning of January, I was at a Bible study. After the Bible study, I was walking back to my car and one of the guys who scoffed at me in the original prayer meeting was walking with me. He started to have his mind changed by the unusually warm weather we were experiencing. As we were walking, he said with a semi-playful expression, "Warm weather we are having," as an obvious reference to the prayer in the fall. It was in the forties that day and as soon as he said that comment it was like a shaft of light went through me, and God spoke to me and said it was about to get really cold. Within two days, the temperature dropped forty degrees and reached a low of one below zero.

With the sudden temperature drop, I was wondering how God was going to handle the situation. A couple of weeks pass by, and I hear through the grapevine that during the time where it got really cold, he got an indoor job for that week! After the cold snap, the temperature returned to the level it was at previously and stayed there for the rest of the winter.

At the end of the winter, I was listening to the radio and a curious announcement caught my attention. The radio announcer said that this was the warmest winter since 1895 when they began keeping records. At that moment I knew God had answered that prayer. I was wondering when I would see the man for whom I prayed for the warm winter. A couple of days pass by, and I went to a men's breakfast sponsored by our church and the man whom I prayed for showed up. I didn't get a chance to talk to him before or during the meeting, but as we were walking out I went up to him and said I heard an interesting thing on the radio, and he stopped me in mid sentence and said he heard the same thing about this being the warmest winter. He was very excited about what God had done, and we talked for some time about what happened. Both of the men that were at the prayer meeting confessed that they scoffed at me and didn't believe me when I told them that God gave me an anointing over the weather when I prayed for a warm winter.

Shown below is a graph of the daily mean (average) temperatures for that winter. The part of the graph surrounded by the outline is when the temperature suddenly dropped forty degrees.

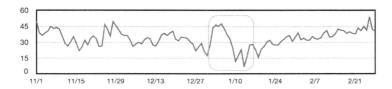

When we look at what happens in the weather, we blindly think weather does what it does without any intervention from God or the devil. Nothing could be further from the truth. We may not understand why things happen the way they do, but you can rest assured that God is in control, and nothing escapes His attention.

Waking up to Jesus

Stefan Raducan

Ever since I can remember my sense of right and wrong was a very strong part of my life and of me. At a very early age I became aware of the existence of God and in that the Holy Trinity itself. Even though there was not a lot of talk about God in my house, I can remember I use to pray. I didn't understand or learn too much about the character of God, except that he was good, perfect, truthful and that He loved me. Also throughout my life I had a reoccurring visiting thought that my life at some point would be transformed in the sense of the lies would be eliminated, being fully guided by the truth, but I never paid much attention to those thoughts.

As I grew up I was going back and forth with my connection with Him, mainly my prayers became inversely proportional with my age and selfish desires, getting to a point where I felt I was in control of the things that I was doing in my life and completely marginalizing God. I grew up in a communist country, where although the country overall was a Christian country, with a strong historical Christian bond, the party's purpose was to destroy any belief in the existence of God. There are many stories of party members even corrupting and infiltrating the church.

My family life was not what you would call a Christian life either. My mother was quite a believer, but my father wasn't. At the age of 14 my family emigrated to the United States after being separated from my father for 4 years and the culture shock and the language itself came with its own hurdles. After some years my parents ended up divorcing too.

In my first year of college, I met my wife to be. The day I saw her my heart, my mind, and my whole life went haywire. I remember any hint of her perfume, or even the highlights in someone's hair resembling hers produced the kind of emotional response that was explosive. We started dating and after 6 years we got married. In the marriage, there was a lot of selfish struggle. As hard as it may sound, I thought that my marriage was the most important thing in my life and the strength of the marriage was based on my stubbornness, fear of failure, and conservative desire to succeed. I loved her in the best way I knew, none the less this love was a selfish love incomparable with the true, unselfish love of Jesus. Due to frequent fights combined with the inability to communicate because of the ingrained worldly beliefs, we always ended up butting heads that would either result in me running away or in character assassination. This combined with my desire to be in control and succeed, my busy job, trying to start a small business, work with my brother on a second career, and on other projects all culminated to the inevitable. My own strength gave up. God gave me into my own iniquities and everything fell apart when I had a nervous breakdown which resulted in leaving home for a month.

After about two weeks I started praying. I vividly remember asking God for help, for someone other then my family or friends who I knew would be partial. I clearly remember looking for the truth and after another two weeks, I started begging God. I was chronically depressed, having been running in overdrive for a very long time. I felt the world crumbled on me. I really missed her, but at the same time I wanted her to suffer and to punish her and to make her realize what "she" was doing. Then I would miss her again, and the whole cycle would restart. I felt completely condemned and lost and was begging God for mercy and help.

One day, I started talking to an old colleague and friend that I had known for 7 years about the troubles I was going through in my marriage and life. In the beginning of my professional career, he was assigned by his boss to be my mentor and show me the ropes at work. I told him about the current events which at the time included her starting the divorce process and his reply was very simple, "Did you ask Him for help?" I felt like a confused kid not even knowing how to respond to the question. The question was totally unexpected as my mind just blanked out.

Months later, my friend told me that God spoke to him the first time he met me that I would be his protégé in that he would teach me the ways of God. He also told me that for the last two weeks God revealed to him that there was trouble on my side. The trust that we build over the years combined with the fact that I independently and specifically prayed to God for an independent and impartial guide, instantly reopened my eyes to Jesus. As I was overwhelmed with all the events I started asking how come he didn't tell me about God before and his response was as modest as the one before "because it wasn't the right time." This great awakening from my long sleep was the beginning of the long transforming journey of learning the truth of God and experiencing a love that is beyond words.

Afraid to Go In

Here is a story of a healing of breast cancer from both a wife and husband's perspective.

Bette Murphy

It had been quite some time since I had been into the doctor for a regular exam, so I was quite uneasy about it. I didn't even have a doctor at the time so that made the decision even more difficult. I finally made an appointment and went in.

The doctor was doing a regular breast examine when she discovered a lump. She asked me to feel the area as well, to see if I could feel the lump, which I did. Since my sister, mom and aunt all had breast cancer and all had mastectomies, I immediately became terrified and began to cry.

The doctor made appointments for a mammogram and an ultrasound to be done the very next day, since I was considered high risk.

On my way home I remember I called my husband, Tim and my sister, Judy to tell them the news as I was very upset.

When I got home I remember getting a phone call from my best friend Linda from high school. We talked a long time and I distinctly remember not telling her what had just happened. I didn't want to worry her, plus it was good getting my mind off of me.

The next day Tim and I went to the doctor for all the tests. I've had mammograms done before but not like this and the same with the ultrasound; completely thorough. Finally they were all done and they had me get dressed and go back to the waiting room till they were done reading the results.

Waiting was a blur to me and it seemed to take hours, but it was actually less than 30 minutes. When they did call us into a room they told us that they had not found anything in my breast. I was completely overjoyed and relieved.

On the way home Tim and I had a very interesting conversation.

Tim Murphy

One day In June 2008 my wife called me on her way home from a doctor's appointment. Bette was very distraught and crying. Her doctor had found a lump the size of a quarter in one of her breasts. I comforted her the best I could, she then hung up and called her sister.

While on her way home I prayed that God would take away her fear. When she got home she was still very upset and talked of the fear she had for breast cancer, as her Mom, Aunt and Sister Carla all had breast cancer and mastectomies.

Bette got a call from her best friend Linda in Georgia and while they talked my heart went out to Bette and I decided to lay hands on her shoulder and pray. I prayed for the Holy Spirit to intercede for her; I did so in a very quiet voice. I then prayed for her in tongues. I did not tell Bette that I had done this and she didn't even notice as she was engaged in her conversation with Linda. I also made a covenant with the Lord not to say anything to Bette unless she was healed, as it was about God, not about me and I wanted all the "Glory" to go to the Lord.

The doctors had scheduled her for tests the next day; a mammogram and an ultrasound imaging. Bette went in for the tests and after about an hour and a half came out waiting for the results. After a short time they called us into an exam room and told us that there was no lump to be found; Bette was unbelievably happy. The mammogram was done in many different angles and nothing was found. The ultrasound was done over and over and nothing was found there either.

Bette was overjoyed with the findings and so I decided I would tell her what the Lord had done for her. We prayed together on the way home and we know that Jesus healed her and we gave Him the glory. It showed us Gods power is still alive and that we must keep faith and always pray. "More prayer, more power".

My Old Car

Stefan Raducan

In the spring of 2002 after many years of hunting for a 6 speed Acura Legend, I finally found one - a 1993 with about 120K miles. This was at a short time after I got married. The car has previously been in an accident. A few years later I myself got in an accident when someone hit me from the back at a stop light. That's when I decided to fix it. While I spent a lot of money, the end job ended costing me more then I originally paid for the car as the car's transmission ended breaking due to the wrong installation of the clutch.

In 2005 I tried putting the car for sale as my wife desired to buy a new car. I had some initial interest after which customer interest went completely dry even as I dropped the price drastically. I had the car for sale for almost a year, at times even growing frustrated with the fact that I couldn't sell it.

Since I bought the car, it's original radio went from bad to worst. It's display completely burned out and towards the end of 2005 it chronically activated the theft alarm when I would turn it on.

In the spring of 2006 as my wife filed for divorce. My Heavenly Father used this experience along with the crumbling of my life, which included losing my job and failing at everything else I was doing, to call me to know and have a relationship with Jesus. A short while later God provided another job for me at about 40 miles distance from my house. My normal commute daily was about two and a half hours.

Since the time I had the car for sale for a while I started despising it. The paint job was so bad that it even started pealing off. One day after about a year in a half of driving a radio-less car that was pealing off paint which at the time had about 180K miles, my friend and Christian mentor mentioned to me that I should start listening to certain christian radio stations. After grumbling to him that my car does not have a radio he said that I should go and buy one. I was very resistant to buying the radio - who in the right mind would buy a radio for a car in this condition. But my friend did not give up. God revealed to him that I should buy a radio and he persisted. Finally I went to Best Buy and it turns out that I had to buy speakers too. With the installation it came to over $700. I was pretty mad for the price since probably the car was worth probably just a little more, but I loved the radio.

God's teaching via the radio

Two and a half hours of preaching daily

Now that I had a radio what was I to do but use it. It turns out that having the usual 30 minutes sermons, I ended up listening to between 2 to 4 sermons a day - my bible learning pretty much sky rocketed. It would really have to be probably a separate book and maybe series of books for me to describe the results of this car radio learning as God used this learning and my experiences to testify to others.

Evolution what?

One night as I was talking to my mother, the subject of evolution came up. I am an engineer by profession. Throughout all my school life I appreciated and liked science. I totally believed that what the school thought about evolution was indeed true. As I was new at the learning of the Word, one thing that God had previously revealed to me is that prayer and being willing to listen makes me able to understand. At the time I felt convicted to pray for understanding and so, I told my mother that I'll pray and see what God will reveal to me about evolution and so I went to my room and did just that. I then went to sleep that night and forgot all about my prayer. In the morning I almost forgot about my dentist appointment setup months in advance. After the appointment, about 2 hours from my regular work drive time, I started listening to Dr. Kennedy on the radio. He had two guests - two micro biologist that, what do you know, were explaining how evolution as explained by Darwin is impossible since the irreducibly complex components that make up a cell and which interact with each other in such a precise pattern could not have evolved from anything else, but indeed were created by God with a specific function in mind. To make matters even more clear, they explained that the most complex thing that human ever created (the engine of a space shuttle) was about as complex as a cell.

Now, I would like to know who can deny that this was the Hand of God, setting up things in such a particular order that His answer to my prayer was undeniable!

Question God = shut car engine off instantly

One morning as I started driving to work, not fully awaken and for some reason feeling pretty grumpy, I turned on my radio and a certain sermon was on. For some reason I didn't like what the pastor was saying and I found myself questioning the things that he was teaching and indirectly, full of pride falling back into my old habits, questioning the validity of the Word of God, whether I truly believed what I believed, and even the existence of God. I must have been about a half a mile away from my house when I started entertaining these thoughts, and the moment I questioned the existence of God, while my car was moving at probably 25 miles per hour, the engine of my car shut off. I was able to park the car, but it did not start until I towed it to the mechanic.

The lesson, zero to humble instantly!

Prayer answered before prayer

At this time in my life God was teaching me about my dependence on Him and His principles. Just recently one of my co-workers and later friend turned his life to Christ after encountering major issues in his marriage. Since I was in the middle of a lengthy divorce which I despised, while waiting on God, He taught me about my failed marriage and how a proper marriage should be like. In one of our early and lengthy conversations, one of the things that I told my friend was that for a marriage to work three people have to make up that marriage - God, the wife and the husband. I also told my friend how all humans are full of pride and sinful, and how the only way for marriage to work is to look at God for guidance and to focus on God while serving the other. In not doing so, we being sinful ourselves would find the spec in others' eyes before seeing the log in our own eyes.

A few months later, one morning as I was driving to work, you would never guess ... a sermon was on. This teaching got me so excited that I even stopped my car to write down the scripture reference. The lesson was about how our most important relationship in our lives is the one we have with Jesus and how we need to focus only on Him. The referenced scripture in this case was the end of the Gospel of John when Peter asks Jesus about his future. After Jesus tells him, Peter then points to John and asks Jesus about John's future. Jesus asks Peter what is it to him if John would live until His return and then tells him to follow what He told him to do. That day my friend invited me to lunch for the first time so he, his son, and I went to lunch. As we were eating, apparently after a discussion he had with his wife a few days ago, my friend reminded me about what I told him moths ago about how we need to focus on God and not on our spouse. He then asked me to give him a scripture reference about this principle. As usual I started getting nervous, but at that time I learned that whenever I got into a tough stressful situation, prayer was the way and so I started praying to God for a scripture reference. Half way through my prayer, it hit me as if God said to me - I already gave you the reference a few hours earlier. I instantly turned to joy, praising the Lord and sharing the events with my friend.

The lesson, God knows about our prayers even before we ask them. If you're not a believer, please explain this exact sequence of events!

Conclusion

After so many years of owning an old car, I really learned to appreciate and love it again. It's old, pealing paint and now even rusting, but it's been a gift from God. He chooses the most unordinary ways to teach and show His Hand on our lives. God is great!

Your Breakers

Brendan Murphy

I was on the phone with my brother and sister-in-law, and we were talking about spiritual matters. At the end of the phone call, I said I'll speak in tongues and you guys interpret and that my brother would interpret the first half and my sister-in-law would interpret the second half. We all agreed and then I spoke in tongues. Then after a brief pause my brother said, "I see waves rolling in like on a beach." My sister-in-law said, "I see a sunrise." We sat there for a couple of minutes wondering what the interpretations meant. We were all scratching our heads and had no clue since it didn't relate to anything we were talking about and didn't relate to anything else. Prophetic utterances can be a powerful, life changing experience where God moves His hand and doors are opened, yet we were all apparently left holding an empty bag. Would I believe that this was from God without any corroborating evidence?

A couple of days pass by and I go out and buy a Christian Jazz CD called, "Double Disc Jazz Praise" containing a double album by John Mehler and Kenneth Nash. I get home and unwrap it and pop it into my stereo, and then I go about my business while I am listing to it. The songs on the CD are all instrumental so there were no words to invoke any internal feelings. The first two songs play through and the music was enjoyable, but nothing remarkable. Then, the third song started playing and I was suddenly gripped from within by the Holy Spirit. It was a simple lyrical melody, but it grabbed me from out of nowhere, and I could tell it was God who was touching my spirit. It had my complete attention since I knew God was trying to tell me something, but what was God trying to tell me through an instrumental song and with this powerful move of the His Spirit? Near the end of the song, it occurred to me that I need to go find out the name of the song, so I grabbed the CD case and read the cover and the name of the song was, "Psalm 42 (Longing For You)." So I thought to myself that I need to read Psalm 42 since God had just placed His finger on me and was trying to get my attention. As I was reading the Psalm, nothing was popping out to me until I reached verses 7 and 8. In those verses it says, "All Your breakers and Your waves have rolled over me. The LORD will command His lovingkindness in the daytime." (Psalm 42:7b-8a) Suddenly I was dumbfounded by what I had read since it matched what was spoken a couple days earlier in the interpretation of tongues. Even of greater importance is that the word came to pass in my life in the intervening years just as God spoke it.

This scripture is a perfect picture of how God works in our lives. The hardships and adversities come and roll over us like waves, yet it is this adversity that molds and shapes us into the image of Christ. Many of us resist the hardships and develop a complaining spirit thinking nothing bad should come upon us now that we are following God. The hardships develop in us a longing for God just as the Psalm says. Without this longing for God, we would drift away from God. We should therefore embrace the waves that God brings over us for He is merciful and knows what He is doing.

Faith in the Silence

Brendan Murphy

Have you ever sat in your house and listened to all the background noise? A modern house has built into it electrical, plumbing, and heating systems and as a result there are motors softly whirring, water flowing through pipes, air flowing through ducts, and countless little machines that are running to make our lives more convenient. All these things add to the background noise of the house, and we become accustomed to it and tune it out. When something causes the power to fail, you become acutely aware of the silence that surrounds you. The feeling is almost eerie in the sense you become dependent on the constant low level background noise.

One day I prayed, "God, teach me to have more faith." When the Holy Spirit comes and dwells within us, there is a peace that cannot be described. He fills us with living water and is constantly reassuring us of the hope we have. The moment I prayed that prayer everything went silent in my spirit, and I felt absolutely nothing like a house that loses its electrical power. I am not saying that God left me, but He chose to be quiet. This silence shrouded me like an impenetrable curtain. Would I believe God was there in the silence? There was no indication from God how long this silence would last, so I walked through this only with the bare knowledge that God is faithful. For three days this silence lasted and then as suddenly as it came, the Holy Spirit again manifested His constant reassurance.

When God was quiet, I learned that we sometimes take for granted His constant diligence over the condition of our souls. When He manifested Himself after the silence, I learned just how potent His presence is in our lives.

"But the righteous will live by his faith." (Habakkuk 2:4)

The Unsuspecting Prophet

Shane Murphy

In the late 80's, I attended a Sunday school class at my church. There was nothing special about the class. It was something I did often. On this particular Sunday morning, I noticed an old friend that I had not seen in five years. He was a staff member of an outreach youth group from a local church, which would later become my home church. His friendship and Christian witness had been instrumental in my salvation seven years earlier when I was just 16 years old. His Christianity seemed very genuine to me. He often opened his home for youth activities. I had great respect for him.

Sometime during the class the Lord spoke to me in a still small voice and said, "Go talk to him. Ask him to get together to talk." The Lord's request was unexpected. I was uncomfortable with the request simply because I was afraid. The Lord did not tell me what we should talk about, just that we should talk. Throughout the remainder of the class, I became increasingly nervous, as I knew the class would soon be over and I would need to talk to him.

What would we talk about if he agreed to meet? I had assumed that the Lord would want the conversation to be about the Baptism of the Holy Spirit. Just a few months prior to that Sunday school class, I had been filled with the Holy Spirit and spoke in tongues. The church I attended did not believe in the baptism of the Holy Spirit, and I had accepted that. It was not my plan to make an issue of it, but if the Lord wanted me to, I would speak to individuals if so directed. It was because of the Baptism of the Holy Spirit that I learned to hear the voice of the Lord, and just as importantly, how to test what I heard. It was this voice that gave me the instruction to talk to my friend.

When the class ended, I went straight to my friend. I said, "Long time since we seen each other. Hey, I would like to get together and talk. I have had some cool things happen to me lately and I would like to tell you about them." Honestly, I expected an excuse or refusal, but to my surprise he immediately agreed. "Yes, that would be great," he said. "Would you like to come to my house tonight?" We set up a time, and then parted ways.

I had the whole day to ponder what the Lord would have me say to my friend. The Lord gave me no instructions and left me to my own imagination. So I crafted plans to tell him how I was baptized in the Spirit, how the Lord healed my girlfriend and another friend, and some other things the Lord had done for me.

I went to his house after dinner. He lived by himself in a small trailer. I was welcomed in and we quickly found ourselves in a couple of chairs. The room was very dark and it felt a bit grim. It was hard to begin. I had no prompting from God on what I should say, so I just began by telling him that the Lord ask me to talk to him during Sunday school that morning. I expected him to be surprised, but he was not. He did not respond at all. I was honest with him and told him I was not sure what to tell him, that I did not know exactly what the Lord's purpose was for this meeting. With nothing else coming to mind, I began to go through the list of testimonies I had worked out that afternoon.

He did not say much while I spoke, other than acknowledging that he was listening. It was a one-sided conversation for a long time. At a lull, he finally interrupted me. I will never forget what he said. He told me that the night before he had been sitting in the very same room considering suicide. He was very honest with God and told Him "God, if you do not send me a prophet, I am going to end my life." He told me details of the loneliness he felt at work, and the fact that he had no one to share his life with. He was a straight talker. I could hear the pain in his voice as he spoke. He felt beaten down with loneliness over the years. He had planned to kill himself that night if God did not respond to his prayers. We talked awhile longer about his pain.

I can't say that any of my words were profound; in fact I knew they were not. It became clear to me as I listened what God's plan was to bring my friend back. It was simply to send me. The only words that mattered that night were when I said, "The Lord sent me." That's it. All he needed was to know that God loved him and that God sent someone to him in that dark hour. The other things I said were of little consequence. I left his house that night with a confirmation from him that things were okay, and I believed him; I could see it in his face.

I did not see him after that night, and the Lord has not crossed our paths since. I heard he met a great lady and was soon married. God knows what is going on in our lives and He answers prayers.

Sister Smith

Pastor Jac Perrin

She looked so old it was hard for me to believe she was really still alive. Perhaps she was in her late seventies, or perhaps younger. Whatever her age, her life had been much harder than what most people had to endure, and I was only a child. To me, even teenagers looked old.

She was called Sister Smith. At least that's what we all called her. Every Sunday morning, on our way to church, our family car would pull up to the curb and at the sound of the horn, she would appear. Descending the old, wooden stairs from a small apartment above an ancient, run-down storefront now inhabited by a bar, I could first see her shoes. They were all white -- just like the ones worn by nurses. They had been carefully polished and cleaned. Like her, they were old, but well kept. Then her ankles and legs next came into view. She had large, strong legs that were covered with white nylons. At about where her shins should be, I would see the hem of her dress. It was all white as well, made of nylon or polyester -- just like the dresses the nurses wore. In fact, all she ever wore was white.

All the white clothing made her skin look darker and her teeth whiter. She smiled a lot. Her face was lined by great, leathery canyons, especially on her forehead and around her mouth. But her smile could light a fire on the coldest of days. She seemed to be such a happy soul who loved children and everyone she ever met.

She smelled fresh and clean. She would squeeze her large body into the backseat of our old Ford so she could get to church. As children, we never minded smashing together to make room for Sister Smith. After all, she always handed out peppermints to the four of us children.

Contrasted with all the white was a big black Bible that seemed about the size of Texas that she carried next to her heart. It was precious to her. As little children, we were precious to her, too. You could just tell that she loved children. She had never had any of her own.

At church, she would sing so enthusiastically as tears rolled into the canyons of her face and down onto her white collar. They seemed to be tears of joy at the new life she had received from Jesus oh so many years ago.

And then after many years, I remember hearing that Sister Smith was very sick and we were going to visit her for the last time. It was a Saturday. It felt unusual because although a Saturday, my parents got all of us kids dressed in our Sunday clothes and pilled us into the car for our last visit to see our angelic friend. Apparently, she was dying.

I cannot remember much about the room. It might have been a nursing home, or perhaps a hospital room. It was too many years ago. My memory has faded like the colors of a beautiful print left too long on the window ledge.

I can remember parts of our last conversation, however. She was lying in bed. It was hard for her to breathe, but she tried so hard to give each of us children a hug and a kiss. After she hugged me, she told me she knew I was going to be a preacher who would lead many people to Jesus. She was so happy about what she had seen in my future. I was not even a teenager. All the ministers I knew were old men. I had a hard time seeing what she so adamantly proclaimed. It just seemed so impossible. She told us she was going to die and go to be with Jesus in Heaven. She described Heaven in vivid color and then she made me promise to meet her there someday, beside the Eastern Gate. She said she would be there waiting to see me again in the new life that was promised to all who believed.

She died sometime soon after that precious meeting.

Years passed and one day I was working with my father. We were on the roof of a local restaurant fixing an industrial air conditioning unit. I had asked dad about Sister Smith and he told me this story as we worked.

He said Sister Smith had been a very bad person in her younger days. She has been a flapper in the 1920's. Flappers were people who lived hedonistically according to whatever appetite happened to tempt them. Where our lives were governed by principles, theirs were governed by appetites.

At that time, it was illegal to make, sell, or drink alcohol. Sister Smith got involved with a group of smugglers who transported whisky from Tennessee up to Iowa where she lived in Des Moines. It was dangerous work, but she excelled at it.

In 1933, when Prohibition ended and alcohol became legal again, Sister Smith was already associated with taverns, saloons, and the folk who ran them. It was now legal for these once furtive associations to do business in the open again. But by the time this change had come, Sister Smith had already moved on to providing another hidden vice to men who lived in the shadows.

Sister Smith had become a prostitute and eventually, even a madam. She provided all kinds of girls to satisfy the sexual desires to the men who frequented the seedy bars and back alleyways of the rough and dangerous East side of Des Moines. She did this successfully for decades. She became known and respected by local organized crime associates and law enforcers alike. By providing discrete services to both the respectable (but not-so-good) and the bad community leaders, without prejudice, she was able to run an illegal business for decades with only infrequent interruptions.

As she got older, the years of hard living, smoking, and drinking began to catch up with her. One day her doctor diagnosed her with terminal cancer. She had a huge tumor at the back of her throat which had spread destruction throughout her body. There was nothing he could do for her. He suggested she go home and get her affairs in order.

Sister Smith was devastated! Her entire life had been a parade of sin, disease, and crime. She understood what it was like to live alone, but the thought of dying alone was more than she could bear. Her only friends shared the common goal of living a life of fun, partying, and moral abandonment. Empathy was not something they were able to offer. None would be interested in the passing of a sick and dying person. There was no fun to be had in something so negative.

As she walked back to her small apartment above the bar, she was lost in her thoughts. She was oblivious to the hot stream of tears that coursed down her cheeks. She knew how to deal with this kind of pain. She would subdue it out with booze. If she had to go, she would go out in style. She would drink herself to death. And so she sat for hours all alone in the back of one of her local hangouts. She let it be known she was not interested in being disturbed. But under the weight of this new information, facing the end of the only life she had ever known, all the noise of the bar interrupted her thoughts. She needed to leave the noise so she could think. And the booze began to sting her sore throat as it passed into her empty stomach.

So after a couple of hours, she decided to go home. At least in the solitude of her tiny room, she would be able to think. But in the darkness of that lonely night, as she made her way home through the cloud of inebriation, she became lost and disoriented. She took a wrong turn and found herself on the wrong block. Where she expected to find the pool hall and bar that stood under her apartment, she instead found a storefront filled with light, and singing, smiling people. It was a small but vibrant storefront church.

At first the light hurt her eyes. She was so used to the darkness, this light made her self-conscious. Part of her wanted to run away back into the shadows, but instead, the loneliness in her heart made her linger near the large glass windows, watching the smiling people inside as they sang and praised. She listened to the words of the songs. The melodies were unfamiliar, but the words appealing. The words were about a man named Jesus who could heal broken hearts, and mend broken lives. They were sung so sincerely with hands raised in the air and a healthy abandon that looked so authentic. It was so unlike the pretense of her world.

Before she knew it, she found herself inside, in front at the altar with two sweet and angelic, young women alongside her. As she called out to God, she felt the weight of her sin being lifted. She felt herself being delivered from the years of sin and pain. All of her evil was released and in a moment, she was healed and made whole. She had no idea precisely how it had happened, but she knew this God/man Jesus had done it and she knew it was real.

It was there on her knees at the altar with her hands raised, speaking in an unknown tongue, releasing all the bad and being overwhelmed by the good that it happened. She saw it as it came through the door she had entered some moments ago and towards her from the back of the room. It was a ball of fire thrown by an unseen hand. Like lightening it flew up the isle and hit her in the mouth. It burned as it found its way into her throat and to the cancerous mass, then diffused throughout every cell of her body.

She immediately knew she was healed! Her body had been healed of cancer. Her mind and soul had been healed of sin.

She never went back to the doctor. She never returned to her old ways. God had healed and cleansed her and told her to wear only white from now on. She would be a nurse to all those around her who were sick and dying from the sins of a misspent life.

Your Testimony

After reading these stories, you may be wondering what does all this mean? If you are a person who has never thought about God, you can use this as an opportunity to investigate the claims of the Bible. From these stories, one can see that God is listening and answers prayers. God's unseen hand moves in our midst and the evidence is there for you to find. In the Bible it says, "You will seek me and find me when you search for me with all your heart." (Jeremiah 29:13) When you open your mind to the possibility that there is a God and He is listening, He will reveal Himself to you in a very personal way. The ability to find God is directly related to your willingness to seek Him. If you seek Him, God will make a way for you to find Him.

From your perspective, you are not guaranteed tomorrow and so your opportunity to reach out to God is today. For God said, "In a favorable time I have answered you, and in a day of salvation I have helped you." (Isaiah 49:8) This moment can be your moment of salvation from the darkness and guilt of your sins and you can be forgiven of the debt of your wrong doings. God sent Jesus from heaven, and He became a child and grew as one of us and then was crucified on the cross to pay the penalty of our sins so that we could enter eternal life through Him.

Here is what the scriptures say about receiving salvation.

For all have sinned and fall short of the glory of God (Romans 3:23)

For the wages of sin is death, but the free gift of God is eternal life in Christ Jesus our Lord. (Romans 6:23)

Jesus said, "For God so loved the world, that He gave His only begotten Son, that whoever believes in Him shall not perish, but have eternal life. For God did not send the Son into the world to judge the world, but that the world might be saved through Him. He who believes in Him is not judged; he who does not believe has been judged already, because he has not believed in the name of the only begotten Son of God. This is the judgment, that the Light has come into the world, and men loved the darkness rather than the Light, for their deeds were evil. For everyone who does evil hates the Light, and does not come to the Light for fear that his deeds will be exposed. But he who practices the truth comes to the Light, so that his deeds may be manifested as having been wrought in God." (John 3:16-21)

For by grace you have been saved through faith; and that not of yourselves, it is the gift of God; not as a result of works, so that no one may boast. (Ephesians 2:8-9)

Jesus said, "I am the way, and the truth, and the life; no one comes to the Father but through Me." (John 14:6)

If you confess with your mouth Jesus as Lord, and believe in your heart that God raised Him from the dead, you will be saved; for with the heart a person believes, resulting in righteousness, and with the mouth he confesses, resulting in salvation. (Romans 10:9-10)

For all who are being led by the Spirit of God, these are sons of God. For you have not received a spirit of slavery leading to fear again, but you have received a spirit of adoption as sons by which we cry out, Abba! Father!" The Spirit Himself testifies with our spirit that we are children of God, and if children, heirs also, heirs of God and fellow heirs with Christ, if indeed we suffer with Him so that we may also be glorified with Him. For I consider that the sufferings of this present time are not worthy to be compared with the glory that is to be revealed to us. For the anxious longing of the creation waits eagerly for the revealing of the sons of God. For the creation was subjected to futility, not willingly, but because of Him who subjected it, in hope that the creation itself also will be set free from its slavery to corruption into the freedom of the glory of the children of God. (Romans 8:14-21)

Don't let this opportunity to know the living God and His Son Jesus slip away from you. God is just one prayer away!

A Tribute to
Our Father

By Shane Murphy

Introduction

John Patrick Murphy died on December 20th, 2017, at the age of 88. My name is Shane Murphy, John's youngest son

This booklet is a compilation of the experience of my family leading up to, and during, our father's final days before he went home to be with the Lord. I gathered input from anyone in my family who was willing to share their experience. For all the stories that I share, I believe there is more that I was not able to capture. I know from the many conversations I had with the family during this time that God was doing wonderful things. My desire is that in reading this booklet you will get a taste of what happened and see the hand of the Lord in all of it. This is a tribute to my families' earthly father, but is also a tribute to our heavenly Father who transformed a sad time in our lives into a very beautiful tapestry.

A note about the poems that you will read in this booklet. In April of 2017, I was in the hospital due to kidney stones that led to a life-threatening kidney infection. Just after being released from the hospital, and out of danger, I felt inspired to write a poem capturing the unexplainable peace I felt while my body was fighting the infection. After that first poem, I continued to write more poems as I felt a leading. I will share three of these poems that relate to my father and his passing.

Who was John P. Murphy?

John had been married 56 years to Kate who died on December 16th, 2008. They had six sons: Tim, Tom, Pat, Sean, Brendan and Shane. Mom cried when I was born because she wanted at least one girl in the family. Dad figured after the third son he didn't have any 'Y' chromosomes to contribute. Mom didn't believe it until the sixth son and would have stopped earlier had she known. Though, don't feel sorry for my mom, as she treated all of her daughter-in-law's as her own.

Dad was a man, like many of his generation, who never said, "I love you" to his sons or hugged them, but his sons had no doubt of his love. He deeply loved his wife. He was a man with a witty sense of humor. It was a pleasure, even our aim, to make dad laugh. Dad had taught his sons to respect God in his efforts of taking us to church. I believe because of this respect, as we grew older, we all developed a relationship with God.

Care of the Aging

Ministering to the elderly is an important part of an individual's obligation to the Lord in honoring their parents. The first poem I wrote was for my brother Brendan, who supported my parents and became their caretaker in their final years. Unmarried, and owner of his own software company, he was able to live in my parent's home and manage the house enabling my parents to remain in their home until their passing. This was a huge blessing for my parents, but it had its share of joy and anguish for my brother. I felt inspired to write this poem titled, "The Care of a Father" as an encouragement to Brendan. In hindsight, I see that this is an encouragement to all caretakers of the elderly.

The Care of the Father

The days have not been forgotten, nor time lost,
in the care of a father for his son,
and the care of a son for his father.
The trees of old stand together as witnesses towering high above the land,
responding to the wind as it pursues its journey.
What is left to be said, or to be done,
in the setting sun is like snow upon the branches of spring.
Upon the altar, a bud establishes its presence,
preparing for the bloom for its glory.
Peace and rest command the moment,
that all stand in awe of the glory of the Lord.

The darkness of night will demand an audience,
but the certainty of the coming dawn brings the footsteps of the Lord,
the coming of the King.

The Role of Our Father

This story begins with the unexpected loss of our mother, Kate, nine years earlier. She had been battling cancer of the blood for many years and far outlived her doctor's prognosis. She had signs of non-debilitating mini-strokes as a result of the medications she was taking. Regardless, mom seemed strong, but on a December afternoon she complained of flu-like symptoms, fell unconscious and was gone before the dawn of the next day. Although the family had been able to gather around her in the hospital, there was no communication with her; though her heart still beat, she was gone. Her body was hours away from shutting down. No goodbyes, or last words. Her death struck the family hard, harder than anyone could have imagined. She was the heart of the family. None of us had felt this devastated before.

It was the years after mom's death I began to see dad's role in our life. If dad would have died before mom, I am sure his son's would not have fully appreciated our father as we have recently. To see him as God saw him. To me, this is a precious gift from God! My mom was the heart of the family, but dad was the foundation. He told all his sons in the last few years that he saw his role early on as just providing for the household, while mom nurtured the family. As a family, we began to see dad as more than just the provider as he claimed.

I wrote a poem called "Jacob's Way" for my father for his 88th birthday on July 1st. I saw my dad like Jacob from the Bible. A man blessed by God, an adventurer and provider.

Jacob's Way

Upon the break of day, a young man awakens into his manhood.

49

His heart stirs deep within that he is to go make a life of his own,
secure in the provision of God.
Committing his strength to the journey he ventures forward.
The path is unknown but the way is clear.
The rising sun releases its brightness to rest on his shoulders
and navigate the way.
For a moment pause is taken, giving way to the breeze of the morning.
The presence of the new day makes itself known whispering the mystery of the
great riches that abound for those who fear God
and acknowledge His ways.
Who can stand in the path of the one blessed by the Lord?
Each step in the journey gives account to the territory
and the borders beyond.
The man, leaving his youth behind, sees that each day will extract its price but
he is not disheartened.
"Favor has followed me like my shadow in the afternoon sun.
All that I have been given, all that I own belongs to you,
oh Lord, the one that I trust.
Though in my youth I contended with you that you would bless me,
I am now content to rest in your shadow".
Faith and blessings together raised the altars that mark the path of the man
who journeyed secure in the provision of God.

Road of Decline

Years before mom died, dad had been diagnosed with a slow
growing form of prostate cancer. While dad's health had ups and
downs over the years, but the decline in his final year was
prominent. The cancer was extracting its price. At the wedding of

one of his grandchildren in May of this final year, all of dad's sons who were at the wedding took advantage of an opportunity to gather around him and pray a blessing. His sons felt an opportunity may not come again as dad's frailty was apparent. In dad's younger years, he would have not thought much of this opportunity, but now he welcomed it, replying to the blessing with a sincere, heartfelt "Thank you boys."

Brendan describes when he noticed the decline. "It all started for me months ago when I saw my dad was gradually declining. I prayed to God and asked that his death would be the greatest act of ministry in his life, a miracle. I also asked that he would die with dignity. Those two prayers were answered. When my mom had died it was really hard. I remember feeling devastated and physically and emotionally wiped out. Later, I wondered how God would get me through the death of my dad in the years to come. God heard me in my wondering and answered me in this time."

Pat describes a much longer road of decline. "I realized as soon as I started writing this tribute that for me my story started shortly after mom died. My relationship with dad deepened after mom passed. That following spring I started to make an effort to drive out to dad's house for lunch and go for long walks every week or so. In those early days, we used to walk 3 miles at a time down to a nearby lake and back. On all these walks, we always talked about mom, the past, present and future. Sometimes we were just silent as we hiked the bike path, enjoying nature. These walks created the one-on-one time with dad that I never had as a child. Back then, dad's main role was to be a provider for the family, while mom took care of the house and the kids. He created great experiences for the family, but making time one-on-one for each of his six boys was hard. So I was grateful to have years of walks and talks with dad, just the two of us. Who would have guessed that God would use this time to heal the inner needs of a young boy? As the cancer progressed the walks got shorter, 3, 2, 1, and then less than a mile. About 2 years ago, I started finding new ways to spend time with dad. We took him to church on Saturday evenings and dinner afterwards fairly often. About every third visit, Dad would ask me whether I had any 'ESP' intuition about him dying. In one of our last visits, I finally said 'Yes.'"

Drawing Down

The first weekend in November, approximately seven weeks before dad died, another grandchild was getting married. There was a groom's dinner where dad and all his sons were invited. I missed the groom's dinner. A photograph was taken of dad surrounded by his sons, then forwarded to me since I was not there. When I looked at the image it was plain to me that death was in dad's face; a darkness I had not seen before. I felt a heaviness of heart. I could not escape this feeling. I was driven to write a poem I named "Strength Draws Down." It took me an hour to write this poem, and I was weeping the entire time. When I finished it, I felt the peace of the Lord and was released from the heaviness.

Strength Draws Down

Strength draws down, the night has arrived, an undisturbed sleep lays invisible
in the darkness but its presence is undeniable.
Silence leads the conversation; memories wait their turn to speak.
Thoughts turn to the Lord, requesting a hearing in His courtyard.
The soul lays prostrate before the King.
Thankfulness sings praises drawing the attention of the host of heaven.
Sorrow turns its face to the heavens and speaks "Come oh Lord, come".
The day was foretold, the hour defined, the Lord's will be done.
The journey has not ended for those who gather.
Hope arises, that which was once built can be built again.
Joy comes knowing the Lord stood at the door
welcoming the sojourner home.

Though the door is now closed, holding back the light of heaven, the fragrance of the Lord remains.
The breath of the Lord is released, a new day is born.

The next day was the wedding. Knowing I would see the whole family, I was not sure who, if anyone, should see my poem. I felt the Lord prompting me to give it to Brendan. During the wedding, I turned to Brendan and with tears being held back I said, "This may be premature, but the Lord said to give you this poem."

Here are Brendan's words regarding the poem. "The first thing that happened was that Shane wrote a poem about my dad's death, and God told him to give it to me first. It was pretty obvious after the first reading of the poem that it was a signal from heaven that God was about to call my dad home. It helped me to deal with feelings of denial and pointing me in the right direction in dealing with the situation. My healing began before it was generally known he was dying. God was helping me come to terms with what He had determined by His own authority in helping me deal with the finality. This gave me strength to do what was needed to be done physically, emotionally, and spiritually."

In the Details

Brendan recounts the circumstances that brought dad to the hospital. "I could see that God was in all of the details everywhere I looked. A week or so before he had gone to the hospital, he made an appointment with a radiation doctor to go over a new treatment that might help him and that happened to be on a Friday. Pat, dad, and myself went to this appointment and we described to the nurse all the symptoms he was feeling and it became alarmingly apparent to the nurse and the rest of us that he needed to be admitted to the hospital. His normal doctor just happened to be in town and working that day, so they got a hold of him. After he had read the notes the nurse took down, he said he would be down right away. When he came and saw my dad, he straight up told him you're dying. We wanted to have him admitted to the hospital so he could get an IV which would perk him up so that people could come and say their goodbyes. The initial blast of this news that he was dying from the doctor was difficult that first day, but God was at work. Each day after that, I actually started getting stronger emotionally and spiritually. This was the hand of God moving to get me through this time as I wondered about after my mom passed away."

God's Priorities

Pat tells how God changed his priorities several weeks before the final decline. He said, "I felt like God 'downloaded' into me a new priority of utmost urgency, and that dad was in his last days. The day I woke up with that direction, Sherrie and I shut down everything; decorating, my consulting work, and anything else to free up time and energy. We had about 2 more weeks with dad after that, and it was the most intimate time we had over the 8 years. We made an effort to do little things. After church one night, he mentioned his toe nails were ingrown and hurting. It was late and he said, 'Maybe next time when you come out you can clip them.' I said 'No, dad, we are going to handle it now.' So Sherrie and I proceeded to find the official glass foot care jar and we spent an hour taking care of all the woes of his feet. Sherrie had the toenail clipper while I held the flashlight and the box cutter to remove callouses ...all under the watchful eye and constant direction of dad every 15 seconds."

Preparing Hearts

Prior to dad's decline, in an effort to help, Sean spoke with dad about trying to keep driving and keep his independence, knowing Pat and his wife Sherrie were coming to drive dad to Mass. Sean said to dad "...otherwise, you would lose your driving ability, end up in the hospital with a fast spiral downward and then you will be put in a nursing home. But, that will not happen." Dad became angry with Sean, but Sean immediately forgave him.

They never spoke of it again acting as if it never happened. After dad's death, Sean mentioned to Brendan what he had said. Then they both realized that it was God who spoke that day where everything happened just as it was said.

Tim and his wife Bette, went through a harrowing experience in October when Bette lost control of her car and drove into open water. Bette, with presence of mind, called Tim as the water surrounded the car. Tim's emphatic words to his wife were "Bette, open the windows! Bette, open the windows!" Bette opened the window, then upon the urging of a bystander on the shore she swam to safety. Shortly after exiting the car, the car submerged. Tim's words had saved Bette. Upon reflection days afterward, Tim broke down crying as the reality overwhelmed him that he almost lost his wife. Tim was not prone to cry, like a lot of men, but with this experience God softened his heart. This gift from God prepared the way for Tim to embrace dad's last days with quiet, intimate moments next to dad's hospital bed.

A Dinner of Thanksgiving

Sean remembers the last Thanksgiving dinner with dad. "Thanksgiving dinner was a spur of the moment type get together. Sarah (Sean's daughter) really wanted an old fashion type dinner so just a few days before the holiday I agreed to do it. Debby (Sean's ex-wife) and her fiancé wanted to come and Pat and Sherrie decided to come at the last minute. I was very ill the day before and had no idea of how this was going to happen. Everyone brought a dish, and everything just worked out somehow. I had all the side dishes in the oven staying warm when I became completely exhausted in severe pain. Pat, Sherrie and Debby took over everything and served up the traditional Murphy buffet. They fixed dad and myself a plate and we ate our Thanksgiving meal together on the couch and this is when dad said something very interesting, 'I feel great peace, the food was wonderful and great.' This was his last full dinner before things went south for him, and he lost his complete appetite and ability to taste anything. He almost finished his plate. I knew in my heart right after he said he felt the peace of God that he wouldn't make it to Christmas. He couldn't eat a full meal or anything even close to it after the Thanksgiving meal."

Brendan's view of the dinner. "When I saw Sean was going to cook a large meal, I knew he would have a difficult time because of his debilitating neuropathy pain which greatly reduces his stamina. So I prayed to God that He would give him strength to make it through the meal. In the middle of Sean preparing the meal I went into the kitchen for the express purpose of finding out how he was doing, and I asked him how he was feeling. He said he was feeling good and not in pain. He made it through making the meal which would have normally wiped him out long before he finished cooking it."

The Final Week Begins

Pat describes the final events that brought dad to the hospital. "Brendan called Sherrie and I because dad couldn't get out of bed. Dad hadn't eaten for two days and was struggling. We were able to bring him back to life with big gulps of Gatorade that night and Thursday so he could make his last doctors appointment on Friday morning. It was at that Friday meeting that the doctor said, 'John you're dying.' With a slight conspiracy and collaboration from the nurses and doctors, they let dad know his organs were shutting down and that there was nothing more they could do. He was checked into the hospital under hospice care 3 hours later. The first thing I did, against the advice of the doctors and nurses, was to insist on a saline IV immediately. The purpose was not to extend his life, but to bring him back long enough so he would be present with the family for the weekend. It was one God inspired weekend with Dad and the family. Dad was fully alert and we got the time we needed with dad. Not only did it wear out dad, it wore me out too. On Sunday, I woke up with the sadness and grief, as it was time to take the IV out. I discussed this with Shane and he was in full agreement and we asked the nurse to stop the treatment."

Band of Brothers

At the beginning of these events, Brendan was talking to a friend about what was happening. The conversation was going in one direction then all of a sudden, the friend made a 90° turn and started talking about "community." He went on very emphatically for two or three minutes on the importance of community and how God uses a community to minister to each other. When he had finished speaking about community, he resumed back on the path of the conversation. This really caught Brendan's attention because it was like God was saying He's going to use all the people involved to minister to each other. As the days had passed, this word about community came to pass.

Perfect Timing

Pat took it upon himself to call all the brother's and family to let them know of dad's condition just after being checked into the hospital. Pat became witness to God's perfect timing. He first called me and I let him know that I would be there in 20 minutes and by the way I have the next two weeks off from work. Next, he called Tom. Tom was scheduled to have both of his knees replaced in mid-December, but to Pat's surprise he learned that Tom's procedure was postponed to the end of January. Tom lives four hours away by car, but this day Tom was actually two miles from the hospital visiting his newly married daughter! Pat's daughter, Katie and her family from South Dakota were in Minneapolis that weekend for another event and were all able to visit and say goodbye to grandpa. Most of dad's visitors came on his second day in the hospital. This was dad's best day because the IV fluids worked wonders to make him alert and welcoming of visitors.

Dad entered the hospital nine years to the day after my mom entered the hospital when she died.

Embracing the Reality

As dad entered the hospital, not all of his sons had accepted in their heart that dad was dying. Hope said to them he would be in the hospital for a short time and then dad would go back to sit in his couch watching TV, as we always found him when people came to visit. In love, the brothers had to look the others in the eyes and say "dad is dying, this is the end of his life, he will not go home again." When the realization had been made, the peace of God followed providing a gentle entrance for grieving to begin.

Tim commented, "It hit me hard even though we all knew he had been deteriorating for some time." He continued, "Seeing him was a joy but it was hard as it was confirmed he did not have much time left. One time I helped raise him and he was probably no more than 120 pounds with his flesh sunk in around his protruding bones. His arms and legs were like twigs or tooth picks."

A Fabulous Day

The second day in the hospital was the big day for visiting. There were plenty of people in dad's room. Pat and Sherrie and my wife and I decided to go get lunch to reduce the congestion in the room. During lunch Pat was reflecting how dismal the day was, namely that dad was deteriorating. I stopped him and said "No! This is a fabulous day." Then, I began to remind every one of the blessings that God has given us. The IV fluids dad had been given created a bubble for dad to feel really good, considering. If fact, if you did not know what was going on, you might think that he would go home from the hospital ready to keep living. Tom and his family were able to visit. Early that morning I had quiet time with dad, with conversations more intimate that I ever had with him. We were in a position to manage dad's pain, and more. Pat, being the family advocate by nature, immediately changed his demeanor and said, "Shane, you're right!"

A Soft Spot for Grandchildren

Tim describes dad, "John had a spot in his heart for the grand kids and was always asking about them." On the third day, Tim's children, Colin and Bryan and their families, came to visit dad. Unfortunately, due to the heavy visiting on the previous day, dad was exhausted. We were also still working to get his pain management correct. Visiting dad was difficult and in fact, the grandchildren had only a few minutes with him. The grandchildren understood and went home. The next day, to my surprise, when I arrived at 7:00 AM. I found Bryan sitting next to dad's bed. In the next couple of hours Colin and his wife, Jen, also came. It was a much better day for dad and there was good interaction between dad and the grandkids.

Tender Mercies

After mom died, dad gave her jewelry to the granddaughter's. This included her wedding ring. In hindsight, dad regretted giving away the wedding ring because he realized what he really wanted is to have their wedding rings buried with him so he could present it to mom when he died. Kristyn (Tom's daughter) was the receiver of the wedding ring and she was told of dad's regret and intention for the rings. During her visit with dad in the hospital, she presented the ring back to him and did it with great joy! Dad was humbled, and extremely grateful.

The first day in the hospital some of the brothers sat down to discuss health care options. At that time, we did not know whether dad had hours or weeks to live. The hospital was just the first, temporary step. We needed to think long term. Dad expressed that he wished to die at home. During the discussion, in unity, the brothers quickly agreed that home hospice was not viable; too much stress on the family. The decision was to make external hospice arrangements. Dad knew the first day he was not going home, and in fact did not really want to leave the hospital. This decision was not up to us, but would be driven by medical guidelines. The plans came together to move dad to a nursing home at 1:00 on the seventh day. This move would have been traumatic for dad because in the last few days dad felt the hospital was his new home because of all the family being there. Dad died on the morning of the seventh day. God provided a tender mercy to lighten our burden.

Suffering Connection

Just before and during the hospital stay, at least three of the brother's unexpectedly experienced pains that lasted into the night, and only to learn later that dad was experiencing that type of pain. For Pat and Tim, it was pain like being beaten up, and deep abdominal pain. For me, this happened a couple of days before dad entered the hospital, where I was short of breath and exhausted. I was all right the next day. I later learned that was the same day dad was struggling, being a short of breath. Tim describes his experience, "When I got home I was sitting on the couch watching TV and I started developing pains in my body. My legs were restless and my shoulders, arms, and back were achy. I took Ibuprofen, yet the pain continued through the night. In the morning, I made my way to the bathroom and I still ached. As I got ready for work, the pains disappeared."

Memories

For the last couple of decades dad struggled with some short-term memory loss. I had fully expected that when his final days came upon him that the memory loss would be exasperated preventing meaningful interaction. I was wonderfully surprised that I was wrong! In the hospital, he still had memory loss, but not any worse than normal. I began to take advantage of the whiteboard in the room to record details dad was interested in knowing but had difficulty remembering. We recorded the medications he was on, the cable channels for his favorite TV shows, etc. This had a very calming effect. At home the night before the sixth day I felt an urgency to bring another whiteboard, as we have filled up the one in the room. There was no way to hang a store bought board. I decided to buy a whiteboard backer, cut it to size, drill holes in the four corners and run rope through the holes. This would be cheap and quick to make and allow me to hang it on the edge of the closet door because of the rope. The next morning, I rushed to the hardware store to obtain the materials. While on the way, Pat called and suggested I get to the hospital sooner than later because dad had a bad night with pain management, and things could go down quickly. Was it worth spending the time on this project if dad died that morning? I struggled with what to do for a few moments, then decided that the whiteboard was important. My plan caused only an one hour delay in arriving at the hospital. I put the whiteboard on the closet door. It worked out just as I had expected. I said to dad "Do you see the whiteboard I made you. We can keep track of everything today." Dad responded "It is for you, I won't need it." My heart sank, thinking I wasted my time. But, throughout dad's last full day before he died, the pain got worse, his anxiety increased, he got demanding on knowing all the details. My gift of the whiteboard became indispensable to help my dad manage this intense day. As a funny side note, I wrote on the whiteboard a checklist of things dad just wanted to remember. First on the checklist I wrote, "Last rights." My wife laughed at me and said I spelled it wrong, it should read "Last rites." I changed it, but realized that "Last rights" might have been more appropriate knowing how dad was very demanding.

Professional Caretakers

I need to take a moment to express my gratitude for the caretakers in the hospital. I know they are trained to help families in end-of-life conditions, but they were a blessing to our family. Our hospital doctor was caring, responsive, seeking ways to help. He explained to us how the body dies which gave us confidence when making medical decisions on when to turn off the IV fluids, which were so effective in providing clarity for dad, but had served its purpose.

The morning my father died the doctor came to his room. He came as soon as he got the death notice. A small group of us were gathered in dad's room to have one last chance to see the body, and say a final goodbye. The doctor told us that the way our family handled the death experience was one of the best he had ever known. His sincerity was clear, as he briefly spoke about losing his father, so we knew he was speaking from experience.

Prayers of the Faithful

If you were to ask my brothers what the greatest privilege was during the time in the hospital, I am certain they would tell you it was their opportunity to pray with dad. For those who wanted, they got their opportunity to lay their hands on dad and pray as if they were in the throne room of heaven. Beyond the prayers that were spoken, I was moved when my brothers expressed their gratitude that they simply had the opportunity to pray for dad.

Tim recounts of time where he and his wife Bette were alone with dad, "It was very touching to us as he told us he had enjoyed a great life, being married to the love of his life Kate for 56 years, raising six boys, and that he had no regrets. We had time, so we asked him if we could pray with him. We laid hands on him and we took turns praying over him. When we were done, we both said we loved him. In typical John fashion he said, 'thank you' rather than 'I love you too.' That was just how Dad was built, very stoic like Bud Grant (NFL football coach)."

Kate is Watching

Brendan brought dad's favorite picture of mom to the hospital to set on the bedside table. Dad always appreciated having the picture of mom, and this time was no different. Seeing the photo, I expected that dad would begin to focus on going home to be with his wife, keeping the photo front and center. But, what I saw surprise me. Instead of focusing on the soon to be reunion with his beloved wife, dad focused on his sons making sure they felt satisfied with the final days with him. He said to Tim on the first night in the hospital "Now is the time for you to get quality time with me before I die." He repeated this comment several times during his stay in the hospital. Dad was caring for his sons until he passed away.

Bible Quiz

Tim was telling a story about having to memorize the Bible verse John 3:16. Dad stopped him, and said, "I don't know that scripture, please tell me the verse." We quoted it for him.

> "For God so loved the world, that He gave His only begotten son, that whoever believes in Him shall not perish, but have eternal life." (John 3:16)

Dad replied, "I really like that verse. My favorite verse is the one where we do not judge each other."

> "Do not judge, and you will not be judged; and do not condemn, and you will not be condemned; pardon, and you will be pardoned." (Luke 6:37)

A few nights later, we revisited this subject with dad and I told him my favorite verse.

> "The conclusion, when all has been heard, is: fear God and keep His commandments, because this applies to every person." (Ecclesiastes 12:13)

Brendan concluded our discussion with the last verse in the Bible.

> "The grace of the Lord Jesus be with all. Amen" (Revelation 22:21).

Dad acknowledged the verses with contentment. I believe that these verses encapsulate the experience we had with our father in his final days.

I Need a Toothbrush

Mary and I were sitting with dad when he decided to eat a little piece of a candy bar in the hope that his energy would return. He could not eat much of the candy bar as it cause him to cough. Worse yet, it left caramel all over his dentures. He needed a toothbrush desperately, so he asked Mary if she could find him one. My wife started a thorough search of the closet, and medical bins that lasted a minute or two. While watching her diligently searching, leaving no stone uncovered, I thought to myself "where would you expect to find a toothbrush?" I got up, walked to the bathroom and saw the toothbrush sitting on the sink. Immediately brought it to dad. Knowing I beat Mary to the punch I said "Here you go dad, I was able to find the toothbrush in a <u>matter of seconds</u>!" I gave my wife a cheesy smile while gloating in my superior tracking skills. After a pregnant pause dad responded, in a tone clearly favoring my wife, "Mary looked longer." He had the last word. Joy rushed into my heart as I contemplated dad's affection towards my wife.

The Big OK

Dad continually needed to wet his lips and his mouth. Early in his stay he was able to drink for himself as long as we had two fingers width of water in a cup. This made it easier for him to drink without spilling in his weakened state. Dad was an engineer by profession, and his training drove him to have the precise amount of water in the cup to make sure he did not spill. In the last few days, dad could no longer wet his own lips. We learned to read his signals on when he needed water, which was when he lifted one finger. We immediately came to his side, dipped a straw into the cup of water, capped the straw with our finger to hold the water and brought it to his mouth. Dad would pull back his lips to expose his teeth, allowing us to release the water where it was needed, at the base of his teeth. Exposing his teeth made me laugh each time because that is what dad's mom would do to her grandchildren to make them laugh many years ago, that is pull back her lips to expose her dentures. It was hilarious. What impressed me about dad was that every time we put water on his lips, he would form the 'OK' sign with his hand saying we got it right. Knowing the pain he was experiencing, I never expected him to be so grateful. To the end, he expressed gratitude for every act of service he received.

Alone with Dad, a Quiet Assurance

Throughout the week, there were times dad just needed to rest. He would say to whoever was watching him to "go home," emphatically saying "I will be okay." Usually, if we were alone with dad, we would respond "No, I will be staying, but I will sit in the chair just on the other side of the curtain." Dad never argued this response. In fact, I personally experienced great joy in keeping watch in the night. Dad told me once that he was grateful I stayed, he just did not want me to be inconvenienced. Mary, my wife, often sat with my dad when the brothers needed to go off and talk. She describes the time as extremely peaceful. Dad expressed his appreciation for her many times. It was the honor of his family to provide dad this quiet assurance.

Several of the brothers really cherished the times to sit with dad alone in the hospital. Pat describes his experiences. "A few times early in the morning and late at night, when the hospital floor was quiet, I sat on his bed instead of the chair and just talked to dad about life, how he felt about dying and how he felt about seeing mom soon."

Through the Pain

As to be expected in end-of-life, dad experienced pain. At times, his pain was enough that he did not like to be touched or hugged. He was gentle as he could be in letting people know not to touch him by raising his hand to signal "Stop, please don't." During a period where his pain was higher, I was joking with him that his hair looked very unkept. "Dad, you have a severe case of 'nap' hair!" Then unexpectedly he requested me to brush it. Brendan had brought some of his personal items a few days earlier, including his brush. I began brushing his hair and I heard him say, "Oh, that feels good." I felt humbled that this simple act was able to give him comfort.

Naked We Came into the World, Naked We Leave

The day before dad passed, Mary and I decided to go home from the hospital around 3:30 in the afternoon. Pat was going to stay for the night, with Sherrie joining him around 5. Usually, someone stayed each night until dad fell asleep for the evening, around 9 PM. Mary and I went out to eat and when we had finished dinner, we decided we would stop by the hospital. We would say "hello" to Pat and Sherrie and see how dad was doing. At 7:45, we walk into dad's room. The room is dark and Pat and Sherri were not there. As I entered the room and passed by the curtain, I see that dad's legs are bare. As I go further I see he has underpants on, but nothing else. Mary stopped in her tracks, then backed out of the room. The closer I got, I saw dad's arms crossed on top of his chest like an Egyptian Pharaoh mummy. He is not wearing a gown. I then checked to see if dad was breathing. Within a moment, I saw that he was breathing comfortably. I walked out of the room, making sure not to wake dad. I saw the nurse. She said my brother had left a few minutes ago. Dad was very hot and was comfortable without his hospital garment on. Dad was hot because his body was entering the final stages of the death process. He died 5 hours later. I was the last person in my family to see dad alive. But, due to God's way of blessing the whole week, there was no regret that we were not by his side when he died. We were content with the circumstances. God changed our focus from dad's death to dad's life.

On the Way Out

Brendan describes his experience in the hour of dad's death.

"When we admitted dad to the hospital there were two names on the emergency call list including my oldest brother Tim and myself. My brother Pat was with me and he wanted his name on the call list also. The nurse put his name on the list and then asked who should be first to be called. Pat suggested putting my name first and so we did. This is important to know for later in the story!

The night dad died, I was trying to fall asleep at home. It was about 1:00 AM. I was in the state where you are half-asleep and half-awake. All of a sudden, I felt a hand grab my right shoulder and gently shake me. This woke me up and stirred my spirit. I turned to my right, and unexpectedly, I saw a face before me. The face was billowing white light so pure and bright, yet it did not hurt my eyes to look at it. I instantly knew it was my dad for I could see some of his face through the light when he woke me up. He did not say anything to me, but he had a huge smile on his face. I could feel the peace of God in a very potent way. Then I lay there for a while wondering what was going on, and then my phone rings at 1:22. I answered the call and it was the nurse from the hospital informing me that my dad just passed away. She says she called me because I was the first one on the list! Amazingly, this was important because my brother Pat has a feature on his phone where he can redirect calls from his cell phone to his land line phone. He forgot to turn this off and if the nurse had called Pat instead of me he would've never answered the call in the middle of the night. God was taking care of the details.

The next morning, I went down to the hospital at 7:00 AM to meet my other brothers and their wives to take care of the details. We were all sitting there and we could feel the peace of God in the room and we were reminiscing about our dad. I told the story of how dad appeared to me in the middle of the night and what happened. They were visibly moved.

When I got home, God told me to tell my brother Sean the testimony of seeing dad in the middle of the night. I walked in and he was sitting on the couch and I told him the story. Then Sean said, 'Do you want to hear a story?' Obviously, I said yes. Sean told me that he prayed the day before that dad would visit the house after he died. Sean said he was disappointed that dad didn't visit him after he heard the news that he died. When he heard my testimony, he connected the dots in his mind. So, what happened to me was a direct answer to what he prayed."

In parallel, one day before dad passed, Sean prayed "Father, please send your holy angels to my dad when he dies and cause a special visitation to happen so that there is absolutely no doubt about my dad's destination in You Lord." The next day Sean told his daughter Sarah about his prayer and the possibility of a visitation from grandpa John. After receiving a text from Brendan in the early morning that dad had died, Sean let Sarah know the news and expressed his disappointment that they didn't have a visit from grandpa. The next day after Brendan had gotten home from the hospital he told Sean about the visitation he had right after dad died. Sean could only say "Praise God!" Sean asked God why he didn't allow him to have a visitation and He responded "Which is better to have, one who had a visit from heaven or the one who prayed for the visitation to happen in the first place?" Sean was humbled and he told God he loved Him.

The Final Day and Last Goodbye

Dad died in the predawn hours of the seventh day. As the sun rose, Pat, Sherrie, Brendan, Mary and I gathered in the hospital room to say our final goodbyes. It was a wonderful time of peaceful fellowship. Tears came readily, but we all realized the burden has lifted, and dad is with the Lord. Pat remembers the morning. "It was hard to take in that dad was actually gone, it looked like he was in a deep sleep. When Sherrie and I got up to leave, and I looked closely into dad's eyes, that's when it hit me dad was gone and God had him."

As the group was getting ready to leave Pat said, "Well, now what?" I spoke up "When mom died I have fond memories of going to Perkins with my kids for breakfast. Anyone interested in going to Perkins?" Everyone liked the idea, and we called Tim and Bette to join us. It turned out to be a joyful time, remembering the week, and beginning to really appreciate all the things the Lord did for the family. It was capped off with Brendan describing the visitation from dad to Tim and Bette.

During this time the realization came to us all, that we can now rest.

Six Days and then God Rested

It struck me that is was significant that dad was in the hospital for six days, and went to be with the Lord on the morning of the seventh day. Ministering work of the Lord occurred each day, with every day being unique. I liken this to the creation story where God created for six days and on the seventh day called his creation finished and then rested. Our family rested on the seventh day.

Journey's End

Pat reflects on the end. "This journey has been hard for me because it combines the grief I never felt for mom and the grief I feel for dad, because now they are both gone. This amazing blessing from God, to experience dad without the barriers of everyday life, of being of intimate service, and all family coming together is the memory I will cherish most."

The brothers were not devastated by dad's death as we were when mom died. Like when a woman's body is prepared for birth, able to endure the pain of birth, God prepared our family for dad's passing.

In the death of my father, God has birthed new life in our family in the form of unity, fellowship, resolution of grief, restoration of family relationships, healing of broken hearts, and the preeminent establishment of God's steadfast love. To me, God played the perfect symphony of His love for our family. I believe the full fruits of events have yet to be fully revealed. Dad's greatest ministry to the family was his final years. This is like when Jesus foretells of his death:

> "Truly, truly, I say to you, unless a grain of wheat falls into the earth and dies, it remains alone; but if it dies, it bears

much fruit." (John 12:24)

My desire in writing this tribute is to encourage you to honor your parents.

> "Honor your father and mother (which is the first commandment with a promise), so that it may be well with you, and that you may live long on the earth." (Ephesians 6:2-3)

Your circumstances will most certainly be different than ours, but in your obedience to God's commandment I believe you will see God move on all of those around you, as He did in our family.

Made in the USA
Columbia, SC
17 March 2018